Memory Quilts

by Linda Causee

LEISURE ARTS, INC.
Little Rock, Arkansas

Produced by

Production Team

Creative Directors:	Jean Leinhauser and Rita Weiss
Photography:	Carol Wilson Mansfield
Book Design:	Linda Causee
Technical Editor:	Ann Harnden

Published by

the art of everyday living
www.leisurearts.com

Library of Congress Control Number: 2013944389
ISBN13: 978-1-4647-1238-8

Introduction

What do you do with all the bits and pieces you have been saving for a lifetime? What do you do with those precious memories? Does anyone look at those old photographs sitting in an album? Are those collected memories of places you visited or events that happened in your life stuffed into dresser drawers never to be seen again?

How about incorporating those precious memories into lovely quilts that could keep someone warm on a cold evening or add warmth to a room hanging on bare walls. That's exactly what we've done in this book. Daddy's little girls are grown up, but what pleasure won't daddy receive when he sees their little faces shining out from a quilt. That beautiful wedding will remain in our minds forever as we see it recreated in a quilt. Those ties that someone's dad wore to work would have been thrown away long ago except that a creative quilter kept them alive by incorporating them into a quilt.

What might happen to your collection of fascinating buttons or beautiful crosses?

Hidden in a drawer where no one can enjoy them, they will soon be forgotten. Why not create a quilt that serves as a lovely background to display their beauty for everyone to enjoy? Even those family recipes stored in an old cookbook can have new life as part of a quilt.

So give your mementos an important place in your life as part of a fantastic quilt. If you only have a few treasures, make a simple wall hanging. If you have a larger collection, you can make a full-size quilt. Whichever size you choose to make, you are creating a place for memories that will last for a long time.

If you've never made a quilt before, or if you're not sure of your quilting ability or your ability to transfer photos to fabric, here are the basic instructions you'll need to become not just a quilter but also a quilter of memories.

I hope you have as much fun as I have had preserving memories for my friends and myself.

Contents

16

Kolacki

Prep Time: 30 minutes   Cook Time: 15 minutes   Total Time: 45 minutes

1 (8-ounce) cream cheese, softened
12 ounces (3 sticks) butter, softened
3 cups all-purpose flour
2 (12-ounce) cans fillings of choice (apricot, prune, raspberry, etc.)
Confectioners' sugar

Preparation:

30

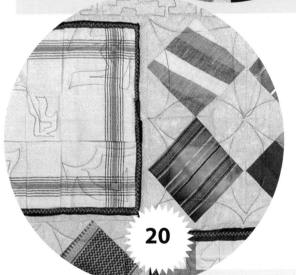

20

34

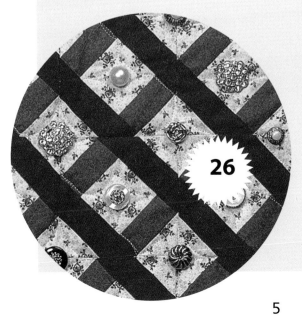

26

38

Wedding of the Stars

Approximate Size: 34" x 34"

For most people wedding pictures sit in an album to be viewed on occasion. For a quilt maker, however, those wedding photos belong in a quilt to be treasured forever.

Materials

12 photos to finish 4" x 4"

1 photo to finish 8" x 8"

*prepared fabric sheets

1 yard blue fabric

1¼ yards black fabric

craft-size batting

1 yard backing

*Purchase prepared fabric sheets or refer to Preparing Fabric for Printing, page 55, to make your own.

Cutting

Photo Blocks

24 squares, 2½" x 2½", blue
24 strips, 1½" x 4½", black
24 strips, 1½" x 6½", black

Center Block

2 strips, 1½" x 8½", black
2 strips, 1½" x 10½", black
2 strips, 1½" x 10½", blue
2 strips, 1½" x 12½", blue

Finishing

2 strips, 2½" x 24½", blue (1st border - sides)

2 strips, 2½" x 28½", blue (1st border- top and bottom)

2 strips, 3½" x 28½", black (second border-sides)

2 strips, 3½" x 34½", black (second border - top and bottom)

4 strips, 2½"-wide, black (binding)

Instructions

Note: *Refer to Printing Photos to Fabric, pages 55 to 57, to transfer your photos to fabric.*

Photo Blocks

1. Adjust photos so that they will finish 4" x 4", then print or copy onto prepared fabric sheets; trim photos to 4½" x 4½".

2. Sew a 1½" x 4½" black strip to opposite sides of a fabric photo. Press strips open. **(Diagram 1)**

Diagram 1

3. Sew a 1½" x 6½" black strip to top and bottom of fabric photo. Press strips open. **(Diagram 2)**

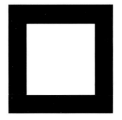

Diagram 2

4. Place a 2½" blue square right side down on upper right corner of photo. **(Diagram 3)**

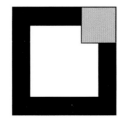

Diagram 3

5. Sew diagonally from upper left to lower right corner of blue square. **(Diagram 4)**

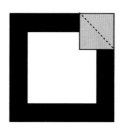

Diagram 4

Hint: *Using a fabric pen or pencil and ruler, draw a line from corner to corner on wrong side of blue squares.* **(Diagram 5)**

Diagram 5

6. Trim ¼" from sewing. **(Diagram 6)**

Diagram 6

7. Flip resulting triangle back and press. **(Diagram 7)**

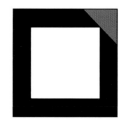

Diagram 7

8. Repeat on lower left corner for Photo Block A. **(Diagram 8)**

Diagram 8

9. Repeat for five more photos.

10. Repeat steps 2 through 7 for remaining 6 photos except place blue squares on upper left and lower right corners of photos for Photo Block B. **(Diagram 9)**

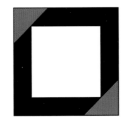

Diagram 9

Center Block

1. Adjust photo so that it will finish 8" x 8", then print or copy onto prepared fabric sheets; trim photo to $8\frac{1}{2}$" x $8\frac{1}{2}$".

2. Sew $1\frac{1}{2}$" x $8\frac{1}{2}$" black strips to opposite sides of fabric photo. Press strips open. **(Diagram 10)**

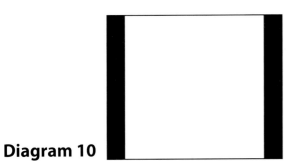

Diagram 10

3. Sew $1\frac{1}{2}$" x $10\frac{1}{2}$" black strips to top and bottom of fabric photo. Press strips open. **(Diagram 11)**

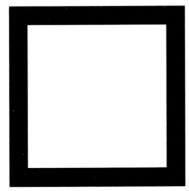

Diagram 11

4. Sew $1\frac{1}{2}$" x $10\frac{1}{2}$" blue strips to opposite sides of fabric photo. Press strips open. **(Diagram 12)**

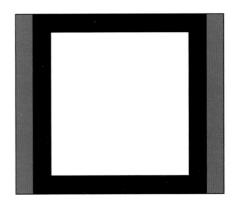

Diagram 12

5. Sew $1\frac{1}{2}$" x $12\frac{1}{2}$" blue strips to top and bottom. Press strips open. **(Diagram 13)**

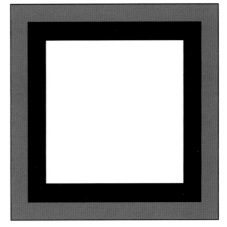

Diagram 13

Finishing

1. Referring to quilt layout, arrange small photo blocks around Center block. Be sure to alternate Photo Blocks A and B.

2. Refer to **Diagram 14** to sew blocks together.

3. Referring to Simple Borders, page 57, add first and second borders.

4. Refer to Finishing Your Quilt, pages 59 to 63, to complete your quilt.

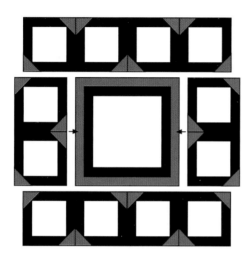

Diagram 14

Wedding of the Stars Quilt Layout

Bonus: Wedding of the Stars Lap Quilt

Approximate Size: 60" x 82"

If you have 24 photos, you can make a lap quilt using the layout below.

Materials

24 photos to finish 8" x 8"

*prepared fabric sheets

2 yards blue fabric

2 ¼ yards black fabric

twin-size batting

4 yards backing

Purchase prepared fabric sheets or refer to Preparing Fabric for Printing, page 55, to make your own.

Cutting

Photo Blocks

24 squares, 4½" x 4½", blue

24 strips, 2½" x 8½", black

24 strips, 2½" x 12½", black

Finishing

7 strips, 2½"-wide, blue (first border)

8 strips, 4½"-wide, black (second border)

8 strips, 2½"-wide, black (binding)

My Religious Jewelry

Approximate Size: 24" x 24"

I have always collected crosses and saints' medals in addition to finger rosaries. While it was comforting to have all of that jewelry in my possession, it was difficult to view the entire collection at the same time. Once I started making quilts, the decision on what to do with the collection was an easy one. Make a quilt and attach the jewelry to the quilt. I made the blocks in the shape of crosses, and I hung a cross in the middle of each quilted cross. Then the saints' medals filled out the empty spaces, and the finger rosaries were placed in the corners. Now I can see my entire collection just by looking at my quilt.

Materials

assorted religious crosses and medals

⅛ yard each of 4 shades of blue

⅛ yard each of 4 shades of yellow

¼ yard very light blue

¼ yard dark blue (binding)

crib-size batting

¾ yard backing

Cutting

Note: *There are two methods for making this quilt: strip piecing or sewing with squares.*

Strip Piecing

3 strips, 1½"-wide, each of 4 shades of blue

2 strips, 1½"-wide, each of 4 shades of yellow

36 squares, 2½" x 2½", very light blue

Squares

45 squares, 1½" x 1½", each of 4 different shades of yellow

54 squares, 1½" x 1½", each of 4 shades of blue

Finishing

3 strips, 2½"-wide, dark blue (binding)

Instructions

Note: *There are two methods for sewing the squares for this quilt: strip piecing or squares.*

Strip Piecing

1. Sew yellow 1 to yellow 2 lengthwise; press seams toward darker yellow. Repeat with yellow 3 and yellow 4. **(Diagram 1)**

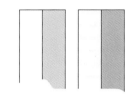

Diagram 1

2. Cut strip sets at 1½" intervals. You will need 90 pairs of squares. **(Diagram 2)**

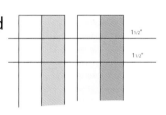

Diagram 2

3. Sew pair 1-2 to pair 3-4 to form a four patch. You will need 45 yellow four patches. **(Diagram 3)**

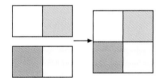

Diagram 3

4. Sew blue 1 to blue 2 lengthwise; press seams toward darker blue. Repeat with blue 3 and blue 4. **(Diagram 4)**

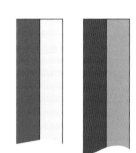

5. Cut strip sets at 1½" intervals. You will need 108 pairs of squares. **(Diagram 5)**

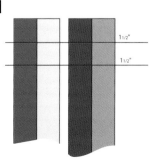

6. Sew pair 1-2 to pair 3-4 to form a four patch. You will need 36 blue four patches. **(Diagram 6)** You will have pairs of squares leftover for border.

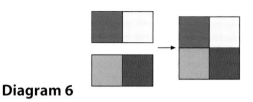

Diagram 6

Squares

1. Sew yellow squares together in pairs; sew pairs together to form yellow four patches. You will need 45 yellow four patches. **(Diagram 7)**

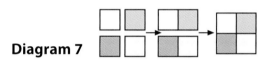

Diagram 7

2. Sew blue squares together in pairs. Sew pairs together to form blue four patches. You will need 36 blue four patches. **(Diagram 8)** You will have pairs of squares leftover for border.

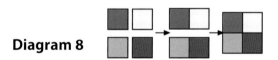

Diagram 8

Cross Nine Patches

1. For rows 1 and 3, sew 2½" very light blue squares to opposite sides of a yellow four patch; repeat. **(Diagram 9)**

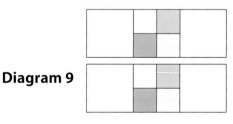

Diagram 9

2. For row 2, sew three yellow four patches together. **(Diagram 10)**

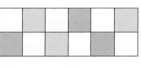

Diagram 10

14

3. Sew rows 1, 2 and 3 together to form Cross Nine Patch. **(Diagram 11)** Repeat for a total of 9 Cross Nine Patches.

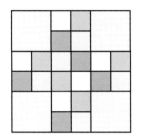

Diagram 11

4. Refer to Finishing Your Quilt, pages 59 to 63, to complete your quilt.

5. Sew assorted jewelry to quilt.

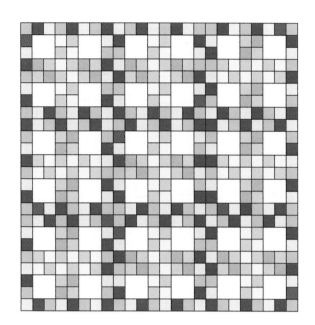

My Religious Jewelry Quilt Layout

Pieced Sashing

1. Sew three blue four patches together. **(Diagram 12)** Repeat for a total of 12 sashing strips.

Diagram 12

Finishing

1. Referring to quilt layout, arrange Cross Nine Patches and pieced sashing in rows. Sew together in rows, then sew rows together.

2. Sew 11 pairs of blue squares together; repeat. **(Diagram 13)**

Diagram 13

Sew to opposite sides of the quilt.

3. Sew 12 pairs of blue squares together; repeat. **(Diagram 14)**

Diagram 14

Sew to top and bottom of quilt.

16

Log Cabin Ties

Approximate Size: 24" x 32"

When I was a little girl, my father went to work every day in a business suit, a shirt and a brightly colored tie. When he retired he took off his tie and announced that he would never wear a tie again. He would have thrown away the ties, but I saved them. For many years they slept in a dresser drawer. One day, I rediscovered the ties and decided to make them into a quilt. They fit perfectly into a pattern for a Log Cabin quilt that will always remind me of my father.

Materials

20 assorted ties

fat quarter red fabric (center squares)

³/₄ yard dark brown fabric (border and binding)

crib-size batting

1 yard backing

4-5 yards lightweight fusible interfacing

Optional: *Foundation or copy paper*

Cutting

Foundation-Pieced Log Cabin

Note: *Although you do not have to cut exact pieces for foundation, you may cut the following strips to make the Log Cabin blocks.*

12 squares, 2" x 2", red

1³/₄"-wide strips, assorted ties

Patchwork Log Cabin

12 squares, 2" x 2", red (1)

12 strips, 1³/₄" x 2", ties (2)

24 strips, 1³/₄" x 3¹/₄", ties (3, 4)

24 strips, 1³/₄" x 4 ¹/₂", ties (5, 6)

24 strips, 1³/₄" x 5 ³/₄", ties (7, 8)

12 strips, 1³/₄" x 7", ties, (9)

Finishing

4 strips, 3¹/₂"-wide, dark brown (border)

3 strips, 2¹/₂"-wide, dark brown (binding)

Instructions

Foundation-Pieced Log Cabin Blocks

1. Make 12 foundations using the pattern on page 19 and referring to Preparing the Foundation, page 48. **(Diagram 1)**

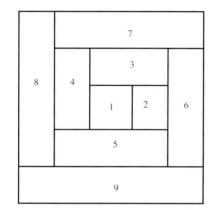

Diagram 1

2. Piece foundation blocks referring to Making the Blocks, pages 49 to 53. **(Diagram 2)**

Diagram 2

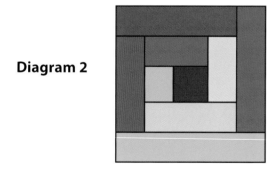

Hint: *Try making the blocks completely random by putting tie fabrics in a bag and pulling out a piece of fabric as you go.*

Note: *Foundation-pieced blocks will finish as a mirror image of the pattern.*

Patchwork Log Cabin Blocks

You can also piece your blocks sewing the cut strips clockwise in numerical order. **(Diagram 3)**

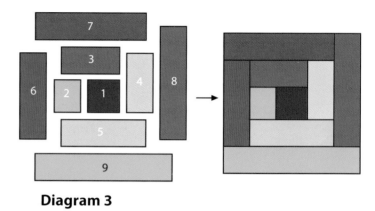

Diagram 3

Finishing

1. Referring to quilt layout, place Log Cabin blocks in four rows of three blocks.

Sew blocks in rows, then sew rows together.

2. Referring to Simple Borders, page 57, add brown border strips.

3. Refer to Finishing Your Quilt, pages 59 to 63, to complete your quilt.

Log Cabin Ties Quilt Layout

Pattern for Foundation Piecing

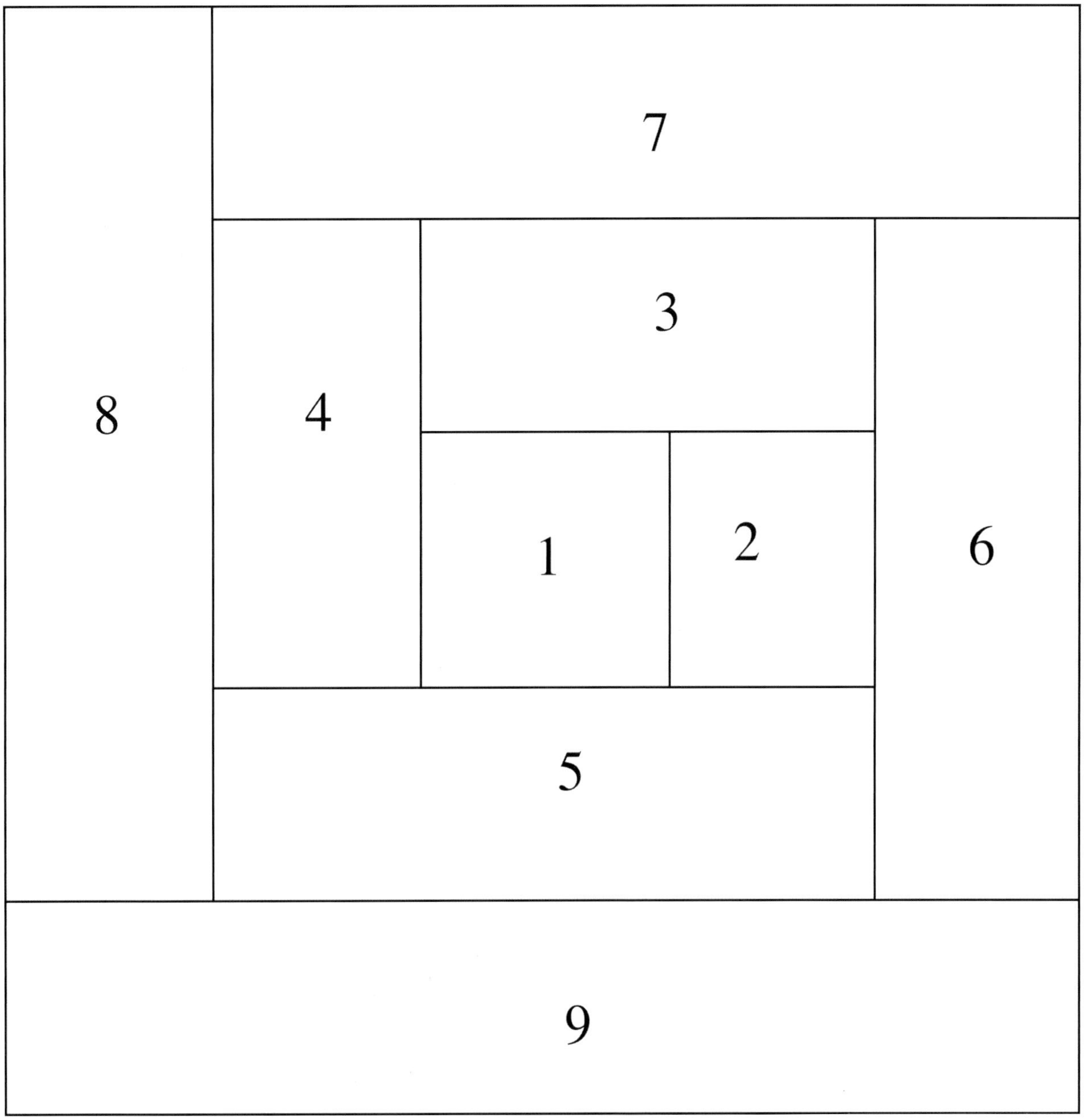

7

3

8 4

1 2 6

5

9

My Daddy's Ties & Handkerchiefs

Approximate Size: 34" x 34"

I couldn't bear to throw away the extra pieces of my father's ties that weren't used in the Log Cabin Ties quilt on page 17. By adding bits of the handkerchiefs my father carried to work in his pocket, I've made another memory quilt.

Materials

5 men's hankies

5 to 8 assorted men's ties

1½ yards beige fabric (background)

½ yard brown fabric (binding)

1-2 yards lightweight fusible interfacing

Optional: *foundation or copy paper*

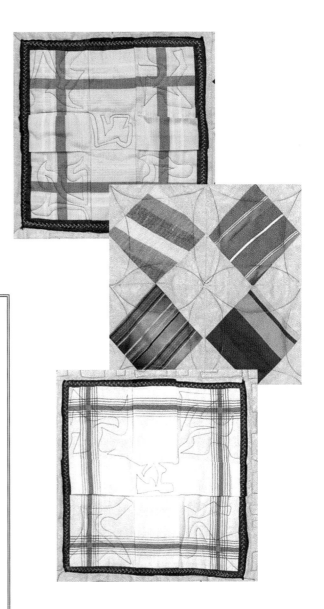

Cutting

Note: *Carefully open seam at back of each tie and press to remove folds. Following manufacturer's directions, iron fusible interfacing to wrong side of pressed ties. Cut squares from the tie fabric.*

5 squares, 10½" x 10½", beige fabric

32 squares, 3½" x 3½", beige fabric (cut in half diagonally)

16 squares, 4" x 4", tie fabric

4 strips, 2½"-wide, beige (border)

4 strips, 2½"-wide, brown (binding)

Instructions

Tie Blocks

Note: *Use foundation piecing, pages 48 to 55, to piece the Tie blocks.*

1. Place tie square to unmarked side of foundation; pin in place.

2. Sew beige triangles to corners of foundation. **(Diagram 1)**

Diagram 1

Repeat for a total of 16 pieced squares.

3. Sew pieced square together in pairs; sew pairs together to complete Tie Block. **(Diagram 2)** Make 4 Tie blocks.

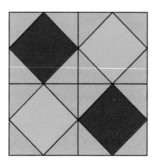

Diagram 2

Hanky Blocks

1. If hankies are larger than the 12½" x 12½" beige squares or if they are not completely square, fold the hanky to fit.

For example, the background square is 12½" x 12½", so your hanky should be 11" square. The hankies used here were 14" x 13". Therefore, fold hanky in half wrong sides together. Sew 1" from fold so hanky will be about 1" shorter than beige square. **(Diagram 3)**

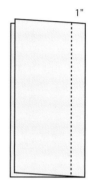

Diagram 3

2. Open hanky and press center section flat being sure the sewn line is centered. **(DIagram 4) Hint:** *Draw a line 1" from fold using a fabric marking pen or pencil.*

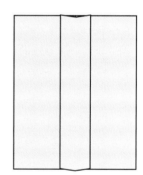

Diagram 4

3. Fold hanky in half in other direction. Sew 1½" from fold. **(Diagram 5)**

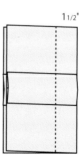

Diagram 5

4. Open hanky and press center section flat being sure the sewn line is centered. **Diagram 6)**

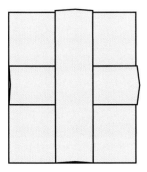

Diagram 6

5. Center hanky on 10½" x 10½" beige square. Sew in place using straight or decorative stitch along edge of hanky. **(Diagram 7)**

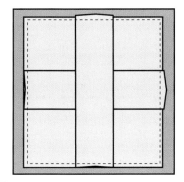

Diagram 7

Repeat for a total of five Hanky blocks.

Finishing

1. Referring to quilt layout, place blocks in rows. Sew blocks together in rows, then sew rows together.

2. Referring to Simple Borders, page 57, sew beige border to quilt top.

3. Refer to Finishing Your Quilt, pages 59 to 63, to complete your quilt.

My Daddy's Ties and Handkerchiefs Quilt Layout

Pattern for Foundation Piecing

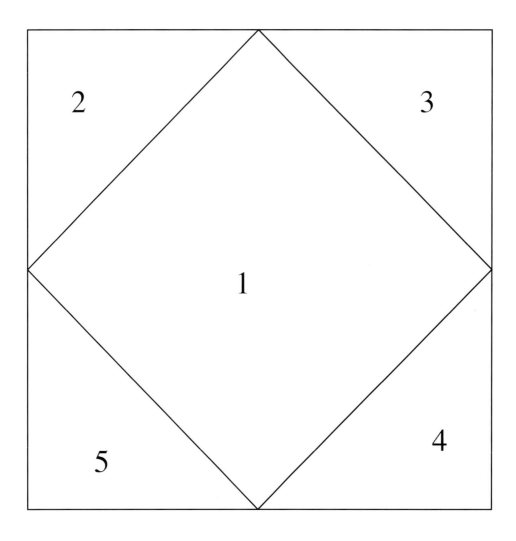

Bonus: My Daddy's Ties and Handkerchiefs Twin-Size Quilt

Approximate Size: 68" x 88"

If you have at least 17 hankies and about 36 assorted ties, you can make a twin quilt using the layout below.

Materials

17 men's hankies

30-36 assorted men's ties

3½ yards beige (background, first border)

1 yard green (second border)

¾ yard brown (binding)

Optional: foundation or copy paper

Cutting

Note: *Carefully open seam at back of each tie and press to remove folds. Following manufacturer's directions, iron fusible interfacing to wrong side of pressed ties. Cut squares from the tie fabric.*

17 squares, 10½" x 10½", beige fabric

144 squares, 3½" x 3½", beige fabric
    (cut in half diagonally)

72 squares, 4" x 4", tie fabric

8 strips, 2½"-wide, beige (first border)

8 strips, 4½"-wide, green (second border)

8 strips, 2½"-wide, brown (binding)

Beautiful Buttons

Approximate Size: 20" x 20"

If like me, you love beautiful buttons, you probably have a collection you can't bear to part with even though the garment upon which they were attached has long been discarded. Create a quilt for the button collection, and you can continue to enjoy them.

Materials

¼ yard light red
⅜ yard dark red
½ yard floral print
craft-size batting
⅝ yard backing
assorted buttons

Cutting

Ribbon Blocks

Note: *Although you do not have to cut exact pieces for foundation piecing, you may cut the following pieces to make the Ribbon Blocks.*

16 squares, 2½" x 2½", floral print

3 strips, 1½"-wide, light red

4 strips, 1½"-wide, dark red

32 squares, 2½" x 2½", floral print (cut diagonally in half)

Finishing

2 strips, 2½"-wide, floral print (border)

2 strips, 2½"-wide, dark red (binding)

Instructions

Ribbon Blocks

1. Make 16 foundations using the pattern on page 29 and referring to Preparing the Foundation, page 48. **(Diagram 1)**

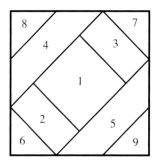

Diagram 1

2. Piece foundation blocks referring to Making the Blocks, pages 49 to 54. **(Diagram 2)**

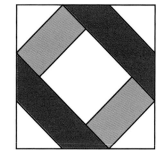

Diagram 2

Finishing

1. Referring to quilt layout, place blocks in four rows of four blocks. Sew together in rows, then sew rows together.

2. Add floral print border following instructions in Simple Borders, page 57.

3. Refer to Finishing Your Quilt, pages 59 to 63, to complete your quilt.

4. Sew buttons on quilt as desired.

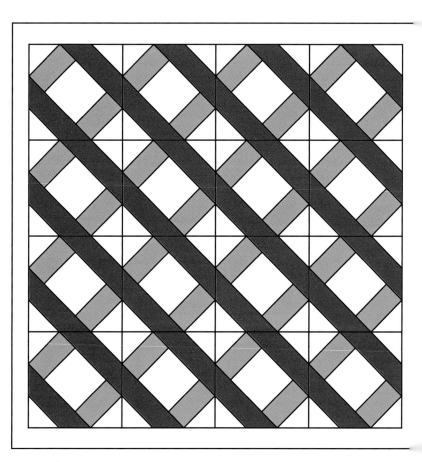

Beautiful Buttons Quilt Layout

Pattern for Foundation Piecing

Note: *Cut patterns apart along dark lines before sewing.*

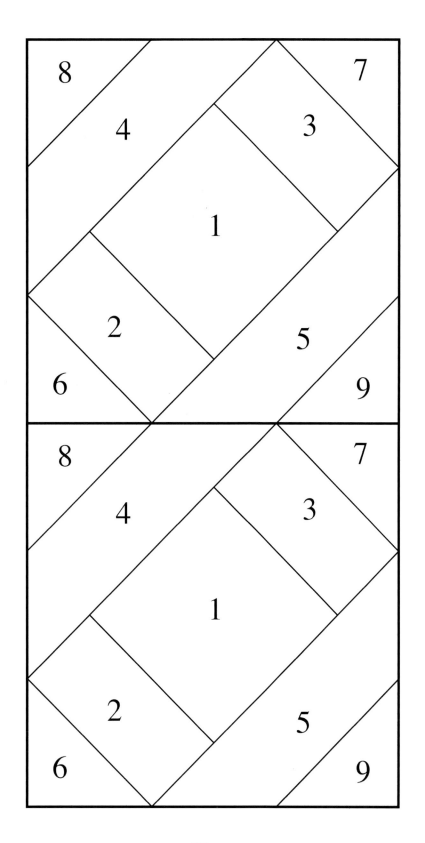

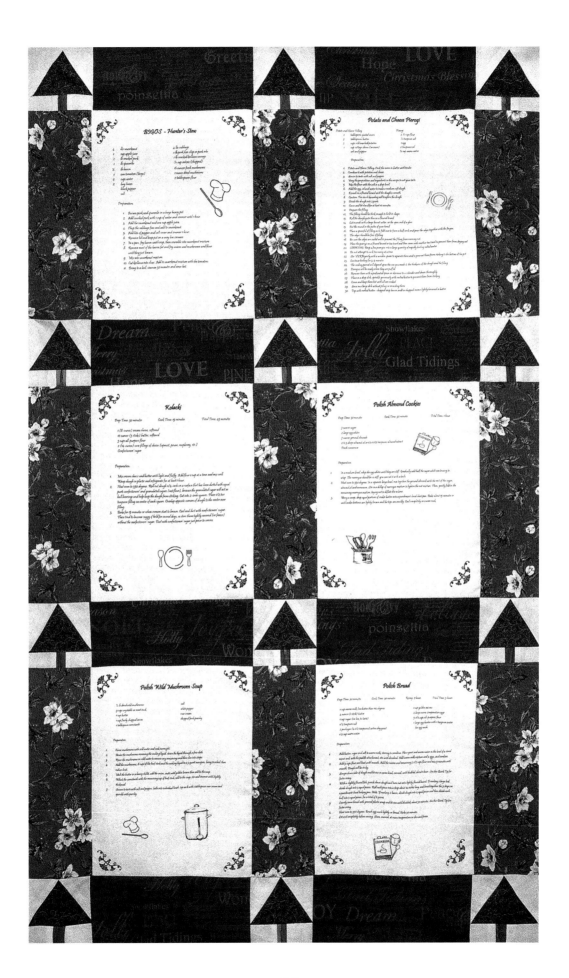

Traditional Christmas Eve Polish Dinner

Approximate Size: 25" x 42"

If it's not enough to just give your family a traditional Christmas Eve dinner, collect the recipes and install them in a quilt. Then when you give your granddaughter the quilt, you'll also add a bit of her heritage. If it's not Polish recipes you want to pass on, make the quilt with a collection of some of your own personal favorites.

Materials

6 favorite recipes (to finish 8" x 10")

*prepared fabric sheets

Foundation or copy paper

fat quarter Christmas print

fat quarter red Christmas floral

fat quarter off-white fabric

fat quarter green fabric

fat quarter brown fabric

craft-size batting

1¼ yards backing

Purchase prepared fabric sheets or refer to Preparing Fabric for Printing, pages 55 to 57, to make your own.

Cutting

Christmas Tree Blocks

Note: *Although you do not have to cut exact pieces for foundation, you may cut the following pieces to make the Christmas Tree blocks.*

12 squares, green

12 strips, brown

24 strips, off-white

12 rectangles, off-white (cut diagonally in half)

Finishing

9 strips, 3½" x 10½", red Christmas floral (vertical sashing)

8 strips, 3½" x 8½", Christmas print (horizontal sashing)

4 strips, 2½"-wide, Christmas print (binding)

Instructions

Fabric Recipes

1. Referring to Printing Photos to Fabric, pages 55 to 57, print recipes to fabric. **Note:** *Type your favorite recipes on the computer and add a few design elements. Center the recipe on the page, then print onto fabric.*

2. Trim the fabric recipes to 8 ½" x 10 ½". **(Diagram 1)**

Diagram 1

Christmas Tree Blocks

1. Refer to Preparing the Foundation, pages 48 to 53, to make twelve foundations using the pattern on page 33. **(Diagram 2)**

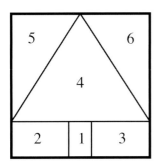

Diagram 2

2. Refer to Making the Blocks, pages 49 to 57, to make 12 Christmas Tree Blocks. **(Diagram 3)**

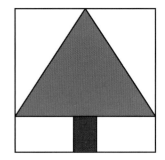

Diagram 3

Finishing

1. Referring to quilt layout, arrange fabric recipes, Christmas Tree blocks, and vertical and horizontal sashing strips. Sew in rows, pressing seams toward sashing strips.

2. Sew rows together.

3. Refer to Finishing Your Quilt, pages 59 to 63, to complete your quilt.

Traditional Christmas Eve Polish Quilt Layout

Pattern for Foundation Piecing

Note: *Cut patterns apart along dark lines before sewing.*

5 6 4 2 1 3	5 6 4 2 1 3
5 6 4 2 1 3	5 6 4 2 1 3
5 6 4 2 1 3	5 6 4 2 1 3

Daddy's Little Girls

Approximate Size: 37" x 34"

When the three sisters were young, the family took many photos, most of which ended up either in albums or dresser drawers. By the time the sisters grew up and had children of their own, the photos were mostly forgotten. When their mother learned that I made memory quilts, she asked me to make a quilt using some of those old photos. Now the three sisters, who never showed an interest in old photos, are trying to decide who gets to keep the quilt.

Materials

twelve photos

*prepared fabric sheets

1½ yards green fabric

1½ yards brown fabric

crib-size batting

1 yard backing

*Purchase prepared fabric sheets or refer to Preparing Fabric for Printing, pages 55 to 57, to make your own.

Cutting

Note: *If your photos are different sizes, you will have to use different size strips to sew to the blocks. Since the Photo Blocks measure 8" x 10" finished and the photos may all be different sizes, you will need to add strips to the photos so that the blocks will end up the same size. Cut all strips the same width, trimming to the correct size.* **(Diagram 1, page 36)**

12 strips, green (widest needed)

9 strips, 1½" x 10½", brown (vertical sashing)

2 strips, 1½" x 35½", brown (horizontal sashing)

2 strips, 1½" x 32½", brown (side borders)

2 strips, 1½" x 34½", brown (top and bottom borders)

4 strips, 2½"-wide, brown (binding)

Instructions

Photo Blocks

1. Referring to Printing Photos to Fabric, pages 55 to 57, print photos to fabric.

2. Place a photo right sides together with a green strip. Sew with a ¼" seam allowance. Press strip open and trim strip even with edge of photo. **(Diagram 1)**

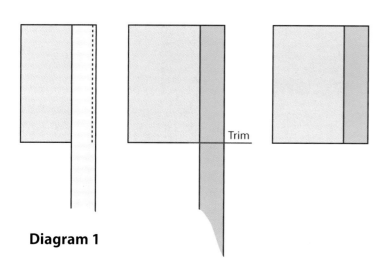

Diagram 1

3. Repeat on opposite side of photo. **(Diagram 2)**

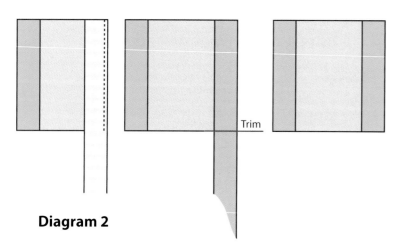

Diagram 2

4. Repeat steps 2 and 3 for top and bottom edges of photo. **(Diagram 3)**

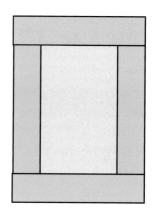

Diagram 3

5. Repeat steps 2 to 4 for remaining photos.

6. Trim block to 8½" x 10".

Note: *Be sure to center the photo when trimming.* **(Diagram 4)**

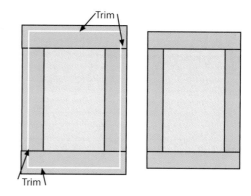

Diagram 4

Finishing

1. Arrange photo blocks in three rows of four blocks.

2. Sew blocks in rows with 1½" x 10½" brown sashing strips in between. **(Diagram 5)**

3. Sew the rows together with 1½" x 35½" brown sashing in between rows.

4. Referring to Mitered Borders, pages 58 to 59, attach border to quilt.

5. Refer to Finishing Your Quilt, pages 59 to 63, to complete your quilt.

Diagram 5

Daddy's Little Girls Quilt Layout

My Favorite Movies

Approximate Size: 58" x 82"

A friend told me about her collection of photos of her favorite movie stars and the films in which they appeared. I thought it was a great idea for a memory quilt so I made her one. Now she can enjoy seeing Christopher Plummer, Spencer Tracy, Lionel Barrymore and Charlton Heston again as well as scenes from her favorite old movies.

Materials

20 assorted photos

*1 t-shirt with patch

**prepared fabric sheets

1½ yards light purple

1½ yards blue

¾ yard dark purple

2 yards turquoise (border, binding)

twin-size batting

4 yards backing

* You can substitute a small photo in place of the t-shirt patch.

**Purchase prepared fabric sheets or refer to Preparing Fabric for Printing, page 55, to make your own.

Cutting

Photo Blocks

20 rectangles, 8½" x 10½", light purple

15 rectangles, 6½" x 8½", dark purple

Finishing

16 strips, 3½" x 10½", blue

12 strips, 3½" x 6½", blue

6 strips, 3½" x 52½", blue

8 strips, 3½"-wide, turquoise (border)

8 strips, 2½"-wide, turquoise (binding)

Instructions

Photo Blocks

1. Referring to Printing Photos to Fabric, page 55, print photos to fabric. **(Diagram 1)**

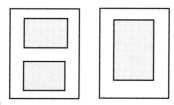

Diagram 1

2. Trim photos along edge of photo. **(Diagram 2)**

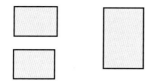

Diagram 2

3. Referring to Using Paper-backed Fusible Web, page 57, iron fabric photos to 8½" x 10½" light purple rectangles. Be sure to center the photos on the rectangle. **(Diagram 3)**

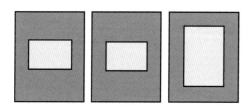

Diagram 3

4. Stitch along edge of photo with a zigzag or your favorite machine embroidery stitch.

5. Fuse t-shirt patch or photo on an 8½" x 6½" dark purple rectangle. Stitch along edge of photo. **(Diagram 4)**

Diagram 4

Finishing

1. Arrange large Photo blocks alternating with 3½" x 10½" blue sashing and dark purple rectangles alternating with 3½" x 6½" blue sashing strips in rows. **(Diagram 5)**

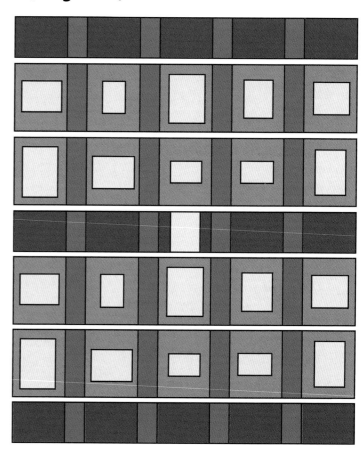

Diagram 5

2. Sew blocks and sashing in rows, then sew rows together with 3½" x 52½" blue sashing strips in between.

3. Referring to Simple Borders, pages 57 to 58, sew 3½"-wide turquoise border to quilt.

4. Refer to Finishing Your Quilt, pages 59 to 63, to complete your quilt.

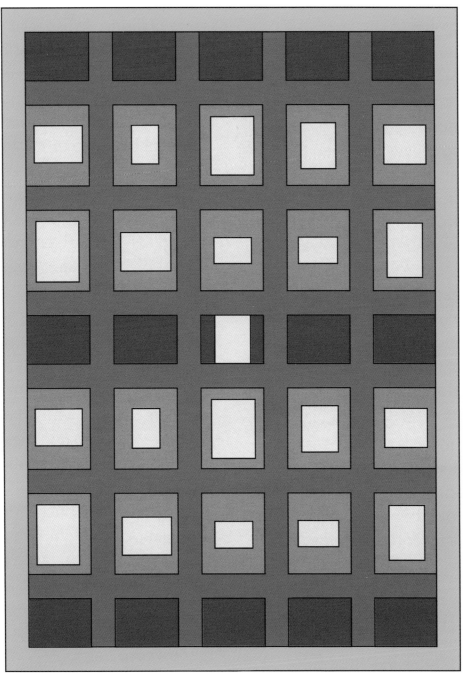

My Favorite Movies Quilt Layout

Making a Memory Quilt

Fabric

For over a hundred years, quilts have been made with 100% cotton fabric, the choice for most quilters.

There are many properties in cotton that make it especially well-suited to quilt making. There is less distortion in cotton fabric, thereby affording the quilter greater security in making certain that even the smallest bits of fabric will fit together. Because a quilt block made of cotton can be ironed flat with a steam iron, a puckered area, created by mistake, can be fixed. The sewing machine needle can move through cotton with a great deal of ease when compared to some synthetic fabrics. While you may find that quilt artists today often use other kinds of fabric, to create the quilts quickly and accurately, 100% cotton is strongly recommended.

Cotton fabric today is produced in so many wonderful and exciting combinations of prints and solids that it is often difficult to pick colors for your quilt. We've chosen our favorite colors for these quilts, but don't be afraid to make your own choices.

For years, quilters were advised to prewash all of their fabric to test for colorfastness and shrinkage. Now most quilters don't bother to prewash all of their fabric but they do pretest it. Cut a strip about 2" wide from each piece of fabric that you will use in your quilt. Measure both the length and the width of the strip. Then immerse it in a bowl of very hot water, using a separate bowl for each piece of fabric. Be especially concerned about reds and dark blues because they have a tendency to bleed if the initial dyeing was not done properly. If it's one of your favorite fabrics that's bleeding, you might be able to salvage the fabric. Try washing the fabric in very hot water until you've washed out all of the excess dye. Unfortunately, fabrics that continue to bleed after they have been washed repeatedly will bleed forever. So eliminate them right at the start.

Now, take each one of the strips and iron them dry with a hot iron. Be especially careful not to stretch the strip. When the strips are completely dry, measure and compare them to your original strip. If all of your fabric is shrinking the same amount, you don't have to worry about uneven shrinkage in your quilt. When you wash the final quilt, the puckering that will result may give you the look of an antique quilt. If you don't want this look, you are going to have to wash and dry all of your fabric before you start cutting. Iron the fabric using some spray starch or sizing to give fabric a crisp finish.

If you are never planning to wash your quilt, i.e. your quilt is intended to be a wall hanging such as many of the quilts in this collection, you could eliminate the pre-testing process. You may run the risk, however, of some future relative to whom you have willed your quilts deciding that the wall hanging needs freshening by washing.

Before beginning to work, make sure that your fabric is absolutely square. If it is not, you will have difficulty cutting square pieces. Fabric is woven with crosswise and lengthwise threads. Lengthwise threads should be parallel to the selvage (that's the finished edge along the sides; sometimes the fabric company prints its name along the selvage), and crosswise threads should be perpendicular to the selvage. If fabric is off grain, you can usually straighten it by pulling gently on the true bias in the opposite direction to the off-grain edge. Continue doing this until the crosswise threads are at a right angle to the lengthwise threads.

Rotary Cutting

Supplies for Rotary Cutting

For rotary cutting, you will need three important tools: a rotary cutter, a mat and an acrylic ruler. There are currently on the market many different brands and types. Choose the kinds that you feel will work for you. Ask your quilting friends what their preferences are, then make your decision.

There are several different rotary cutters now available with special features that you might prefer such as the type of handle, whether the cutter can be used for both right- and left-handed quilters, safety features, size, and finally the cost.

Don't attempt to use the rotary cutter without an accompanying protective mat. The mat will not only protect your table from becoming scratched, but it will protect your cutter as well. The mat is self-healing and will not dull the cutting blades. Mats are available in many sizes, but if this is your first attempt at rotary cutting, an 18" x 24" mat is probably your best choice. When you are not using your mat, be sure to store it on a flat surface. Otherwise your mat will bend. If you want to keep your mat from warping, make certain that it is not sitting in direct sunlight; the heat can cause the mat to warp. You will not be able to cut accurately when you use a bent or warped mat.

Another must for cutting accurate strips is a strong straight edge. Acrylic rulers are the perfect choice for this. There are many different brands of acrylic rulers on the market, and they come in several widths and lengths. Either a 6" x 24" or a 6" x 12" ruler will be the most useful. The longer ruler will allow you to fold your fabric only once while the smaller size will require folding the fabric twice. Make sure that your ruler has ⅛" increment markings in both directions plus a 45-degree marking.

Cutting Strips With a Rotary Cutter

Before beginning to work, iron your fabric to remove the wrinkles. Fold the fabric in half, lengthwise, bringing the selvage edges together. Fold in half again. Make sure that there are no wrinkles in the fabric.

Now place the folded fabric on the cutting mat. Place the fabric length on the right side if you are right-handed or on the left side if you are left-handed. The fold of the fabric should line up along one of the grid lines printed on the mat. **(Diagram 1)**

Right-handed

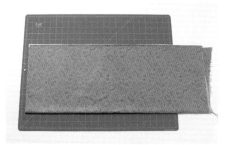

Left-handed

Diagram 1

Straighten one of the cut edges first. Lay the acrylic ruler on the mat near the cut edge; the ruler markings should be even with the grid on the mat. Hold the ruler firmly with your left hand (or, with your right hand if you are left-handed). To provide extra stability, keep your small finger off the mat. Now hold the rotary cutter with blade against the ruler and cut away from you in one quick motion. **(Diagram 2)**

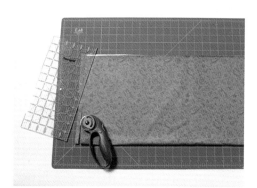

Diagram 2

Carefully turn the fabric (or mat with the fabric) so the straightened edge is on the opposite side. Place the ruler on the required width line along the cut edge of the fabric and cut the strip, making sure that you always cut away from you — never toward you. Cut the number of strips called for in the directions. **(Diagram 3)**

Diagram 3

After you have cut a few strips, you will want to check to make certain that your fabric continues to be perfectly square. To do this, just line up the crosswise markings along the folded edge of fabric and the lengthwise edge of the ruler next to the end of fabric you are cutting. Cut off uneven edge. If you fail to do this, your strips may be bowed with a "v" in the center, causing your piecing to become inaccurate as you continue working.

Cutting Squares and Rectangles

Now that you have cut your strips, you can begin to cut squares or rectangles. Place a stack of strips on the cutting mat. You will be more successful in cutting — at least in the beginning — if you work with no more than four strips at a time. Make certain that the strips are lined up very evenly. Following the instructions given for the quilt, cut the required number of squares or rectangles. **(Diagram 4)**

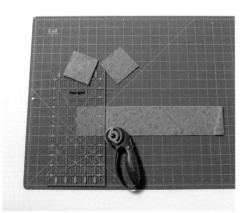

Diagram 4

Cutting Triangles

Once your squares are cut, you can cut triangles, including half-square triangles and triangle squares.

Half-Square Triangles

The short sides of a half-square triangle are on the short grain of the fabric. This is especially necessary if the short edges are on the outer side of the block.

Cut the squares the size indicated in the instructions, then cut the square in half diagonally. **(Diagram 5)**

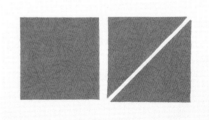

Diagram 5

Triangle Squares

These are squares made up of two different-colored triangles. To make these squares, you can cut individual triangles as described in Half-Square Triangles above. Then sew two triangles together. A quick method, especially if you have several triangle squares with the same fabric, is to sew two squares together. Then draw a diagonal line on the wrong side of the lighter square. Place two squares right sides together and sew ¼" from each side of the drawn line.

Cut along the drawn line, and you have created two triangle squares. **(Diagram 6)**

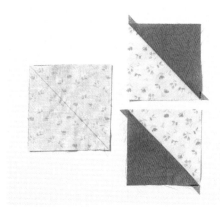

Diagram 6

Stitch and Flip

This is a method for quickly creating triangles and octagons or trapezoids.

Instead of cutting these shapes, cut and sew squares or rectangles together. **(Diagram 7)**

Diagram 7

With right sides together, place a small square in the corner of a larger square or rectangle. Then sew diagonally from corner to corner of the small square. **(Diagram 8)**

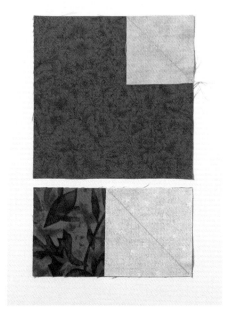

Diagram 8

Trim the corner about ¼" from the seam line. **(Diagram 9)**

Diagram 9

Flip the triangle over and iron.
(Diagram 10)

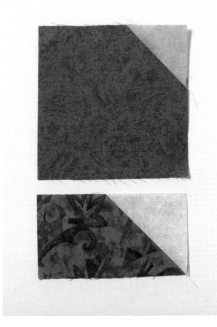

Diagram 10

Repeat at the other corners.
(Diagram 11)

Diagram 11

Strip Piecing

Strip piecing is a much faster and easier method of making quilts rather than creating the blocks piece by piece. With this method, two or more strips are sewn together and then cut at certain intervals.

For instance, if a block is made up of several 3" finished squares, cut 3 ½"-wide strips along the crosswise grain. **(Diagram 12)**

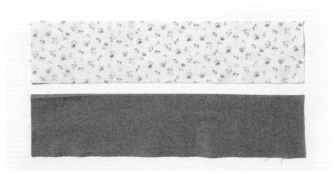

Diagram 12

With right sides together, sew two strips along the length. The seam should be pressed to the dark side of the fabric. **(Diagram 13)**

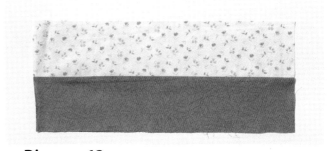

Diagram 13

Cut across strips at 3½" intervals to create pairs of 3½" squares. **(Diagram 14)**

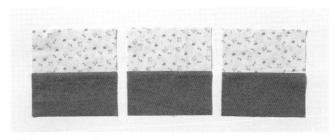

Diagram 14

Foundation Piecing

Materials

Before you begin, decide the kind of foundation on which you are planning to piece the blocks.

Paper

The most popular choice is paper. It's readily available and fairly inexpensive. You can use copy paper, newsprint, tracing paper—even computer paper. The paper does not remain a permanent part of your quilt, as it is removed once the blocks are completely sewn.

Fabric

If you choose to hand piece your block, you may want to choose fabric as your foundation. Just remember that fabric is not removed after you make your block so you will have another layer to quilt through. This may be a problem if you are planning to hand quilt. Using fabric might be an advantage, however, if you want to use some non-traditional quilting fabrics, such as silk or satin, since the fabric foundation will add stability to the block. Fabric makes a good choice for crazy quilts. If you do decide to use fabric, choose a lightweight and light-colored fabric, such as muslin, that will allow you to see through for ease in tracing.

Other Materials

Another option for foundation materials is Tear Away™ or Fun-dation™, translucent non-woven materials combining both the advantages of both paper and fabric. They are easy to see through, but like paper they can be removed with ease.

Currently a new kind of foundation material has appeared in the market place: a foundation paper that dissolves in water after use. Two companies, W.H. Collins and EZ Quilting by Wrights, are producing this product.

Preparing the Foundation

Place your foundation material over your chosen block and trace the block pattern. Use a ruler and a fine-line pencil or permanent marker, and make sure that all lines are straight. Sometimes short dashed lines or even dotted lines are easier to make. Be sure to copy all numbers. You will need to make a foundation for each block you are planning to use.

If you have a home copier, you can copy your tracing on the copy machine. Since the copy machine might slightly alter the measurements of the block, make certain that you copy each block from the original pattern.

You can also scan the block if you have a home scanner and then print out the required number of blocks.

Cutting the Fabric

In foundation piecing, you do not have to cut perfect shapes!

You can, therefore, use odd pieces of fabric: squares, strips, rectangles. The one thing you must remember, however, is that every piece must be at least ¼" larger on all sides than the space it is going to cover. Strips and squares are easy: just measure the length and width of the needed space and add ½" all around. Cut your strip to that measurement. Triangles, however, can be a bit tricky. In that case, measure the widest point of the triangle and cut your fabric about ½" to 1" wider.

Other Supplies for Foundation Piecing

Piecing by hand:

You will need a reasonably thin needle such as a Sharp size 10; a good-quality, neutral-colored thread such as a size 50 cotton; some pins, a glue stick; fabric scissors; muslin or fabric for the bases.

Piecing by machine:

You will need a cleaned and oiled sewing machine; glue stick; pins, paper scissors, fabric scissors, foundation material.

Before beginning to sew your actual block by machine, determine the proper stitch length. Use a piece of the paper you are planning to use for the foundation and draw a straight line on it. Set your machine so that it sews with a fairly short stitch (about 20 stitches per inch). Sew along the line. If you can tear the paper apart with ease, you are sewing with the right length. You don't want to sew with such a short stitch that the paper falls apart by itself. If you are going to use a fabric foundation with the sewing machine, use the stitch length you normally use since you won't be removing the fabric foundation.

Using a Pattern

The numbers on the block show the order in which the pieces are to be placed and sewn on the base.

It is extremely important that you follow the numbers; otherwise the entire process won't work.

Making the Blocks

The important thing to remember about making a foundation block is that the fabric pieces go on the unmarked side of the foundation while you sew on the printed side. The finished blocks are a mirror image of the original pattern.

Step 1: Hold the foundation up to a light source—even a window pane—with the unmarked side facing. Find the space marked 1 on the unmarked side and put a dab of glue there. Place the fabric right side up on the unmarked side on Space 1, making certain that the fabric overlaps at least ¼" on all sides of space 1. **(Diagram 15)**

Diagram 15

Step 2: Fold the foundation along the line between Space 1 and Space 2. Cut the fabric so that it is ¼" from the fold. **(Diagram 16)**

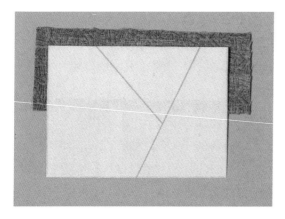

Diagram 16

Step 3: With right sides together, place Fabric Piece 2 on Fabric Piece 1, making sure that the edge of Piece 2 is even with the just-trimmed edge of Piece 1. **(Diagram 17)**

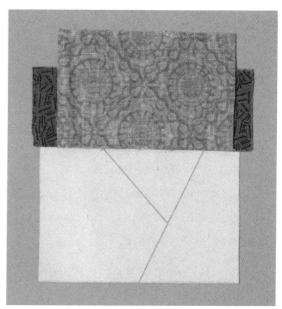

Diagram 17

Step 4: To make certain that Piece 2 will cover Space 2, fold the fabric piece back along the line between Space 1 and Space 2. **(Diagram 18)**

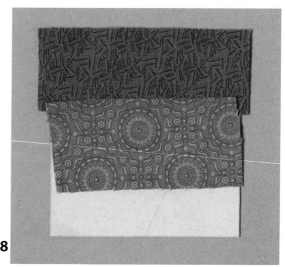

Diagram 18

Step 5: With the marked side of the foundation facing up, place the piece on the sewing machine (or sew by hand), holding both Piece 1 and Piece 2 in place. Sew along the line between Space 1 and Space 2. **(Diagram 19)**

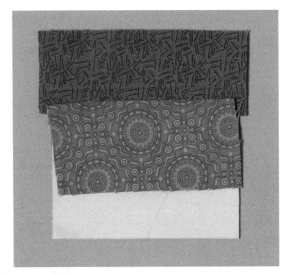

Diagram 20

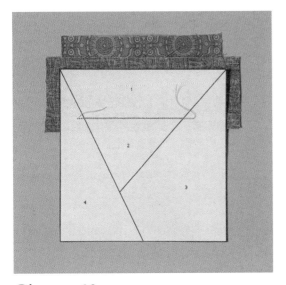

Diagram 19

If you use a small stitch, it will be easier to remove the paper later. Start sewing about two or three stitches before the beginning of the line and end your sewing two or three stitches beyond the line. This will allow the stitching to be held in place by the next round of stitching rather than by backstitching.

Step 6: Turn the work over and open Piece 2. Finger press the seam open. **(Diagram 20)**

Step 7: Turning the work so that the marked side is on top, fold the foundation forward along the line between Space 1+2 and Space 3. Trim about $\frac{1}{8}$" to $\frac{1}{4}$" from the fold. It is easier to trim the paper if you pull the paper away from the stitching. If you use fabric as your foundation, fold the fabric forward as far as it will go and then start to trim. **(Diagram 21)**

Diagram 21

Step 8: Place Fabric #3 right side down even with the just-trimmed edge. **(Diagram 22)**

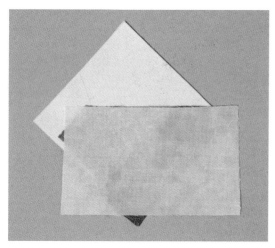

Diagram 22

Step 9: Turn the block over to the marked side and sew along the line between Space 1+2 and Space 3. **(Diagram 23)**

Diagram 23

Step 10: Turn the work over, open Piece 3 and finger press the seam. **(Diagram 24)**

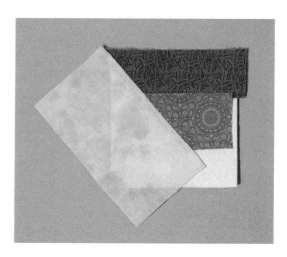

Diagram 24

Step 11: In the same way you have added the other pieces, add Piece #4 to complete this block. Trim the fabric ¼" from the edge of the foundation. The foundation-pieced block is completed. **(Diagram 25)**

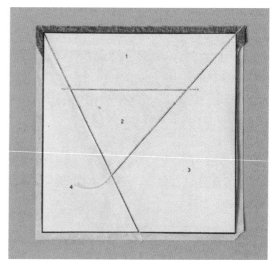

Diagram 25

After you have finished sewing a block, don't immediately remove the paper. Since you are often piecing with tiny bits of fabric, grainline is never a factor. Therefore, some of the pieces may have been cut on the bias and may have a tendency to stretch. You can eliminate any problem with distortion by keeping the paper in place until all of the blocks have been sewn together. If, however, you want to remove the paper, stay stitch along the outer edge of the block to help keep the block in shape.

Sewing Multiple Sections

Some blocks in foundation piecing, such as *Beautiful Buttons*, are created with two or more sections. These sections, which are indicated by letters, are individually pieced and then sewn together. The cutting line for these sections is indicated by a bold line. Before you start to make any of these multi-section blocks, begin by cutting the foundation piece apart so that each section is worked independently. Leave a ¼" seam allowance around each section.

Step 1: Following the instructions above for Making the Blocks, complete each section. Then place the sections right sides together. Pin the corners of the top section to the corners of the bottom section.
(Diagram 26)

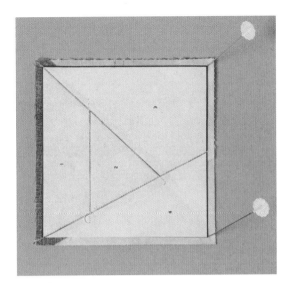

Diagram 26

Step 2: If you are certain that the pieces are aligned correctly, sew the two sections together using the regular stitch length on the sewing machine. **(Diagram 27)**

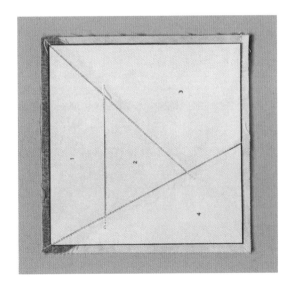

Diagram 27

Step 3: Press the sections open and continue sewing the sections in pairs. **(Diagram 28)**

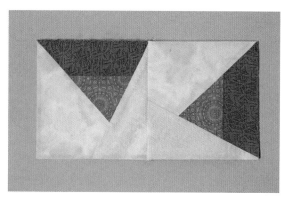

Diagram 28

Step 4: Sew necessary pairs of sections together to complete the block. **(Diagram 29)**

Diagram 29

The blocks are now ready to sew into your quilts.

What You Don't Want to Forget

1. If you plan to sew by hand, begin by taking some backstitches which will anchor the thread at the beginning of the line. Then use a backstitch every four or five stitches. End the stitching with a few backstitches.

2. If you plan to sew by machine, start stitching two or three stitches before the start of the stitching line and finish your stitching two or three stitches beyond the end.

3. Use a short stitch (about 20 stitches per inch) for paper foundations to make it easier to remove the paper. If the paper falls apart as you sew, your stitches are too short.

4. Finger press (or use an iron) each seam as you finish it.

5. Stitching which goes from a space into another space will not interfere with adding additional fabric pieces.

6. Remember to trim all seam allowances at least ¼".

7. When sewing points, start from the wide end and sew towards the point.

8. Unless you plan to use it only once in the block, it is a good idea to stay away from directional prints in foundation piecing.

9. When cutting pieces for foundation piecing, never worry about the grainline.

10. Always remember to sew on the marked side, placing the fabric on the unmarked side.

11. Follow the numerical order, or it won't work.

12. Once you have finished making a block, do not remove the paper until the entire quilt has been finished unless you stay stitch around the outside of the block.

13. Be sure that the ink you use to make your foundation is permanent and will not wash out into your fabric.

Printing Photos to Fabric

Purchased Fabric Sheets

By far the easiest method for transferring photos onto fabric is to purchase prepared fabric sheets. There are several on the market: June Tailor Colorfast Computer Printer Fabric (white or cream); Printed Treasures fabric sheets; and Inkjet Transfer Paper by TransferMagic.com. Just download your digital photos onto your computer or scan printed photos. Then re-size the photos to fit the project and print onto the fabric sheets following the manufacturer's directions.

Preparing Fabric for Printing

Although purchased fabric sheets are easy to use, they can be very costly especially if you have several items to print onto fabric. To prepare your fabric for printing, you will need high-quality 100% cotton fabric, Bubble Jet Set 2000, square plastic tub, rubber gloves, freezer paper, rotary cutter, mat and ruler, and Bubble Jet Rinse.

Step 1: Use high quality 100% cotton such as Kona Cotton by Robert Kaufmann. The fabric should be at least 200 threads per inch. Cut the fabric into rectangles, 9" x 11$\frac{1}{2}$" which is slightly larger than a sheet of paper.

Step 2: Pour a little of the Bubble Jet Set 2000 into a square plastic tub. The Bubble Jet Set will allow the ink of your inkjet printer to bond permanently with your fabric.

Step 3: Place a fabric rectangle into the plastic tub. Wearing a pair of rubber gloves, push the fabric into the liquid until it is soaked through. Add another fabric rectangle, add a little more Bubble Jet set 2000 and thoroughly saturate the fabric. Continue this process until you have treated all the fabric needed for your project.

Step 4: Let the fabric air dry by hanging or lay the fabric on a table covered with plastic. Pour any leftover Bubble Jet Set liquid back into the bottle for the next use.

Step 5: When the fabric rectangles are completely dry, iron to the shiny side of freezer paper. Be sure that there are no air bubbles between the fabric and freezer paper. Also, do not overheat the fabric and freezer paper or you will lose the bonding ability.

Step 6: Trim the sheets to 8½" x 11". Be sure to use a sharp rotary cutter. Trim any loose threads hanging from the fabric edges.

Step 7: Change your printer settings to the highest DPI and the media type setting to high gloss photo paper. Print photos.

Step 8: Let the printed pages set at least 24 hours then rinse with Bubble Jet Set Rinse. The rinsing step is important because it removes excess ink so the pictures don't run during subsequent washings. You do not need to heat set with an iron.

Using Transfer Paper to Transfer Photos to Fabric

Photos can also be printed onto fabric using transfer paper, good-quality cotton fabric, and a hot iron.

Step 1: Reduce or enlarge photo as needed for your particular project and print onto transfer paper following manufacturer's directions.

Step 2: Trim off any excess paper from the edges of your photo.

Step 3: Heat iron to cotton or linen setting.
Hint: *For best results, use an iron without steam vents to ensure even transferring.*

Step 4: Place cotton fabric right side up on a hard work surface such as a counter or solid table covered with a pad or heat-resistant cover. An ironing board could be too unstable. Place transfer face down onto pressed fabric aligning photo with grain of fabric.
Hint: *Cover transfer with tissue before pressing to protect fabric from yellowing when exposed to hot iron.*

Step 5: Place iron on top of the transfer and press down hard. Wait five or six seconds (depends upon temperature of iron) and move the iron to another section. Continue until the entire transfer has been set. Be sure to lift and move the iron, not push it across the transfer as that can cause shifting.
Hint: *You may need to do a trial run to get the correct heat setting and length of heat time for your iron.*

Step 6: Once you have heated the entire transfer, immediately remove the paper by pulling away with the grain of the fabric. Do not remove the transfer paper at a diagonal since that can cause distortion of image.
Hint: *If the paper doesn't come off easily, re-iron the transfer and pull away while hot. If the transfer cools too much, it becomes difficult to remove.*

Using Paper-backed Fusible Web

Appliquéing with paper-backed fusible web is an easy and quick way to attach fabric shapes to a background fabric. Use a lightweight product so that your needle does not get gummed up when machine sewing the edges.

Step 1: Trace pattern onto the paper side of the fusible web. Rough cut pattern shape.

Step 2: Position fusible web pattern with paper side up onto wrong side of fabric; fuse in place with hot iron. **Note:** *Refer to manufacturer's directions for heating setting and pressing time for the product you are using.* Cut out along drawn line. Repeat for all patterns.

Step 3: Position fusible appliqué pieces onto background fabric as shown in the project instructions. Fuse into place following manufacturer's instructions.

Step 4: Using a machine zigzag stitch and matching or invisible thread, stitch along all raw edges of appliqué pieces. **Hint:** *Practice on another piece of fabric to see which zigzag width and length works best for you.*

Making a Quilt

Sewing the Blocks Together

Once all of the blocks for your quilt have been made, place them on a flat surface such as a design wall or floor to decide on the best placement.

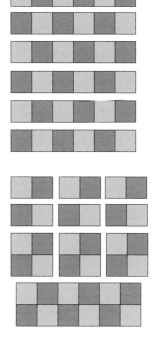

Sew the blocks together. You can do this by sewing the blocks in rows, then sewing the rows together; or, sew the blocks in pairs then sew pairs together. Continue sewing in pairs until entire quilt top is sewn together. **(Diagram 30)**

Diagram 30

Adding Borders

Borders are usually added to a quilt sides first, then top and bottom.

Simple Borders

Step 1: Measure the quilt top lengthwise and cut two border strips to that length by the width measurement given in the project instructions. Strips may have to be pieced to achieve the correct length. To make the joining seam less noticeable, sew the strips together diagonally. Place two strips right sides together at right angles. Sew a diagonal seam. **(Diagram 31)**

Step 2: Trim excess fabric ¼" from stitching. **(Diagram 32)**

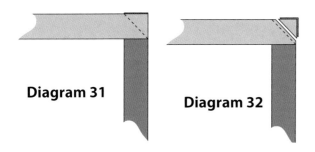

Diagram 31

Diagram 32

Step 3: Press seam open. **(Diagram 33)**

Diagram 33

Step 4: Sew strips to the sides of the quilt. Now measure the quilt top crosswise, being sure to include the borders you have just added. Cut two border strips, following the width measurement given in the instructions.

Step 5: Add these borders to the top and bottom of the quilt. Repeat this process for any additional borders. Use the ¼" seam allowance at all times and press all of the seams to the darker side. Press the quilt top carefully.

Mitered Borders

Mitered borders are much more time-consuming, but sometimes the results may well be worth the effort.

Step 1: Measure the quilt top lengthwise. Cut two strips that length plus twice the finished border width plus ½" for seam allowances. Piece if necessary, referring to Step 1 in Simple Borders on page 57.

Step 2: Measure the quilt top crosswise. Cut, piecing if necessary, two strips that length plus twice the finished border width plus ½".

Step 3: Find the midpoint of border strip by folding strip in half. **(Diagram 34)**

Step 4: Place strip right sides together with quilt top matching midpoint of border with midpoint of quilt side. Pin in place. **(Diagram 35)**

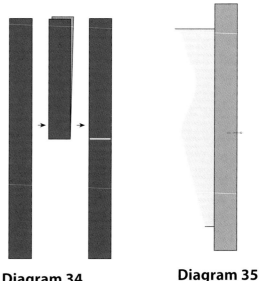

Diagram 34

Diagram 35

Pin border to quilt top along entire side.

Step 5: Beginning ¼" from top edge, sew border strip to quilt top, ending ¼" from bottom edge. Backstitch at beginning and ending of sewing. **(Diagram 36)**

Step 6: To finish corners, fold quilt top in half diagonally right sides together; borders will extend straight up and away from quilt. Place ruler along folded edge of quilt top going into border strip; draw a diagonal line on the border. **(Diagram 37)**

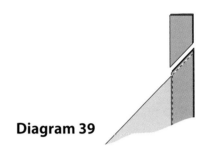

¼"

¼"

Diagram 36

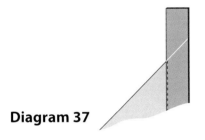

Diagram 37

Step 7: Beginning at corner of quilt top, stitch along drawn line to edge of border strip. **(Diagram 38)**

Diagram 38

Step 8: Open quilt at corner to check miter. If satisfied, trim excess fabric ¼" from diagonal seam. **(Diagram 39)**

Diagram 39

Step 9: Repeat process on remaining three corners.

Finishing Your Quilt

Attaching the Batting and Backing

There are a number of different types of batting on the market today including the new fusible battings that eliminate the need for basting. Your choice of batting will depend upon how you are planning to use your quilt. If the quilt is to serve as a wall hanging, you will probably want to use a thin cotton batting. A quilt made with a thin cotton or cotton/polyester blend works best for machine quilting. Very thick polyester batting should be used only for tied quilts.

The best fabric for quilt backing is 100% cotton fabric. If your quilt is larger than the available fabric you will have to piece your backing fabric. When joining the fabric, try not to have a seam going down the center. Instead cut off the selvages and make a center strip that is about 36" wide and have narrower strips at the sides. Seam the pieces together and carefully iron the seams open. (This is one of the few times in making a quilt that a seam should be pressed open.) Several fabric manufacturers are now selling fabric in 90" or 108"-widths for use as backing fabric.

It is a good idea to remove the batting from its wrapping 24 hours before you plan to use it and open it out to full size. You will find that the batting will now lie flat when you are ready to use it.

The batting and the backing should be cut about one to two inches larger on all sides than the quilt top. Place the backing wrong side up on a flat surface. Smooth out the batting on top of this, matching the outer edges. Center the quilt top, right side up, on top of the batting.

Now the quilt layers must be held together before quilting, and there are several methods for doing this:

Safety-pin Basting: Starting from the center and working toward the edges, pin through all layers at one time with large safety pins. The pins should be placed no more than 4" apart. As you work, think of your quilting plan to make sure that the pins will avoid prospective quilting lines.

Thread Basting: Baste the three layers together with long stitches. Start in the center and sew toward the edges in a number of diagonal lines.

Quilt-gun Basting: This handy trigger tool pushes nylon tags through all layers of the quilt. Start in the center and work toward the outside edges. The tags should be placed about 4" apart. You can sew right over the tags, which can then be easily removed by cutting them off with scissors.

Spray or Heat-Set Basting: Several manufacturers have spray adhesives available especially for quilters. Apply these products by following the manufacturers' directions. You might want to test these products before you use them to make sure that they meet your requirements.

Fusible Iron-on Batting: These battings are a wonderful new way to hold quilt layers together without using any of the other time-consuming methods of basting. Again, you will want to test these battings to be certain that you are happy with the results. Follow the manufacturers' directions.

Quilting

If you like the process of hand quilting, you can—of course—finish these projects by hand quilting. However, if you want to finish these quilts quickly, in the time we are suggesting, you will want to use a sewing machine for quilting.

If you have never used a sewing machine for quilting, you may want to find a book and read about the technique. You do not need a special machine for quilting. Just make sure that your machine has been oiled and is in good working condition.

If you are going to do machine quilting, you should invest in an even-feed foot. This foot is designed to feed the top and bottom layers of a quilt evenly through the machine. The foot prevents puckers from forming as you machine quilt. Use a fine transparent nylon thread in the top and regular sewing thread in the bobbin.

Quilting in the ditch is one of the easiest ways to machine quilt.

This is a term used to describe stitching along the seam line between two pieces of fabric. Using your fingers, pull the blocks or pieces apart slightly and machine stitch right between the two pieces. The stitching will look better if you keep the stitching to the side of the seam that does not have the extra bulk of the seam allowance under it. The quilting will be hidden in the seam.

Free-form machine quilting can be used to quilt around a design or to quilt a motif. The quilting is done with a darning foot and the feed dogs down on the sewing machine. It takes practice to master Free-form quilting because you are controlling the movement of the quilt under the needle rather than the sewing machine moving the quilt. You can quilt in any direction—up and down, side-to-side and even in circles—without pivoting the quilt around the needle. Practice this quilting method before trying it on your quilt.

Attaching the Continuous Machine Binding

Once the quilt has been quilted, it must be bound to cover the raw edges.

Step 1: Start by trimming the backing and batting even with the quilt top. Measure the quilt top and cut enough 2 ½" wide strips to go around all four sides of the quilt plus 12". Join the strips end to end with diagonal seams and trim the corners. **(Diagram 40)** Press the seams open.

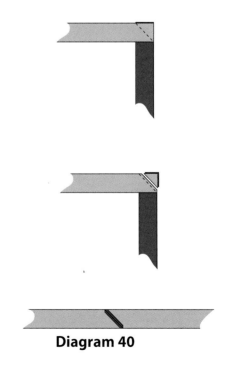

Diagram 40

Step 2: Cut one end of the strip at a 45-degree angle and press under ¼". **(Diagram 41)**

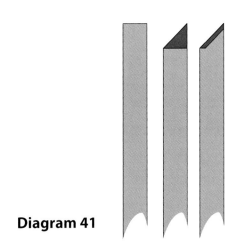

Diagram 41

Step 3: Press entire strip in half lengthwise, wrong sides together. **(Diagram 42)**

Step 4: On the back of the quilt, position the binding in the middle of one side, keeping the raw edges together. Sew the binding to the quilt with the ¼" seam allowance, beginning about three inches below the folded end of the binding. **(Diagram 43)**

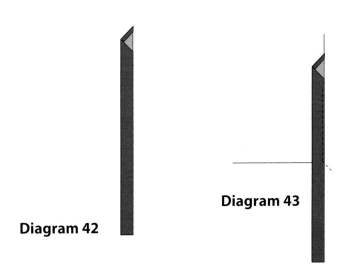

Diagram 43

Diagram 42

At the corner, stop ¼" from the edge of the quilt and backstitch.

Step 5: Fold binding away from quilt so it is at a right angle to edge just sewn. Then, fold the binding back on itself so the fold is on the quilt edge and the raw edges are aligned with the adjacent side of the quilt. Begin sewing at the quilt edge. **(Diagram 44)**

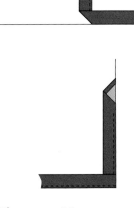

Diagram 44

Step 6: Continue in the same way around the remaining sides of the quilt. Stop about 2" away from the starting point. Trim any excess binding and tuck it inside the folded end. Finish the stitching. **(Diagram 45)**

Diagram 45

Step 7: Fold the binding to the front of the quilt so the seam line is covered; machine-stitch the binding in place on the front of the quilt. Use a straight stitch or tiny zigzag with invisible or matching thread. If you have a sewing machine that does embroidery stitches, you may want to use your favorite stitch.

Adding a Rod Pocket

In order to hang your quilt for family and friends to enjoy, you will need to attach a rod pocket to the back.

Step 1: Cut a strip of fabric, 6" wide by the width of the quilt.

Step 2: Fold short ends of strip under ¼", then fold another ¼". Sew along first fold. **(Diagram 46)**

Diagram 46

Step 3: Fold strip lengthwise with wrong sides together. Sew along raw edges with a ¼" seam allowance to form a long tube. **(Diagram 47)**

Diagram 47

Step 4: Place tube on ironing surface with seam up and centered; press seam open and folds flat. **(Diagram 48)**

Diagram 48

Step 5: Place tube on back of quilt, seam side against quilt, about 1" from top edge and equal distance from side edges. **(Diagram 49)**

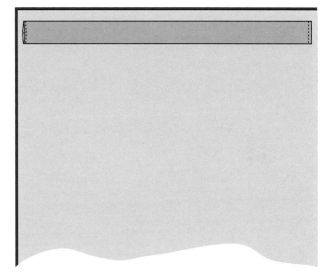

Diagram 49

Pin in place so tube is straight across quilt.

Step 6: Hand stitch top and bottom edges of tube to back of quilt being careful not to let stitches show on front of quilt.

Labeling Your Quilt

Always sign and date your quilt when finished. You can make a label by cross-stitching or embroidering or even writing on a label with a permanent marking pen on the back of your quilt. If you are friends with your computer, you can even create an attractive label on the computer.

Index